Aurora

aurora

SHARON THESEN

Coach House Press

Published with the assistance of the Canada Council, the Ontario Arts Council, the Department of Canadian Heritage and the Ontario Publishing Centre.

With gratitude I acknowledge Michael Ondaatje, Robin Blaser, Jenny Penberthy, Kathleen Fraser, Josephine Jungic, Renee Rodin, and Bob Sherrin for their conversation, encouragement, and suggestions. Special thanks to Michael Redhill for editing the ms.

Cover Illustration: Guido Reni, detail from *Aurora* (1613), fresco. Courtesy of the Amministrazione Maria Camilla Pallavicini, Rome. All rights reserved.

Bibliography, discography:
William Shakespeare, *A Midsummer Night's Dream*
Michele Leggott, *Dia*
Richard Grossinger, *Planet Medicine*
Sister Marie Keyrouz, *Hymns to the Virgin Mary*
Clarissa Pinkola Estés, *Women Who Run With the Wolves*
Sun Ra, "Space is the Place"
Nat King Cole Trio, "When I Take my Sugar to Tea"
John Donne, "Air & Angels"
Billie Holiday, "This Year's Kisses"

First Edition
Printed in Canada
1 3 5 7 9 8 6 4 2

Canadian Cataloguing in Publication Data

Thesen, Sharon, 1946–
Aurora

Poems.
ISBN 0–88910–471–9

I. Title.

PS8589.H47A87 1995   C811'.54   C95–930764–8
PR9199.3.T54A87 1995

Aurora is dedicated to my son Jesse Charles Fawcett.
And to Frances Boldereff Phipps.

We live on a planet of seas and vapors, mud, fire, and dust. We are suspended in a field of attractions cast by heavy objects which go on eternally, nesting in each other so that the smallest things we know are in continual touch and influence from the largest and from things beyond visibility.

Richard Grossinger

heart like mine

Michele Leggott

Gala Roses

and when she weeps,
weeps every little flower

I DRIVE THE CAR

 I drive the car
while the choir ascends
toward a far transparency
these words tap at
with a show of politeness

I drive my car
and my friend also drives hers
& takes a detour to watch crows assemble
& disperse over the Cassiar Connector

They hang out there

I drive the car
afraid of the earthquake
  & drive it
afraid of myself, what is it I
do, I wonder, & also what
others do, are they also
afraid?

Or else go crazy I drive the car
around in that
too, like a maniac   like the wind

In the car someone's playing the piano
with an eye-patch on & the helium
voice of a drugged-out poet, Besame Mucho,
& mucho federales
at the border

Where you can't step out
past a certain point painted
with certitude across the pavement &
why would you want to, anyway,
enter that foreign country
all aplomb & curiosity

14

No, I drive the car.
I hope it works that the engine
don't fall apart. I think
oh, it will last five or ten years.
Then what. Another car.

My car I drive back & forth
around the town over bridges & here
and there, like everyone else
driving their cars. In the back seat
sits the ghost of your grandma.

I drive the car & pick up my friend
at her house, she comes out
the red door, I'm five minutes late
& we're laughing tragically by the time we
go past the SPCA.

The road is black after dark rain
and it ends in the sea. Big semis
are minotaurs, some have smoke-stacks.
The air stings from tiny black particles
they blow at it, burdened and in a hurry

I put her in drive
& then I drive her & this
is what I do, I drive
the car.

HOW IT WAS

The guy across the alley's
old red weathervane with yellow
letters at the four winds is missing the figure
of the blue sailor who in foul weather
tore around on top smoking a pipe.

I was out in that weather dabbing suet
on tree branches for the starlings.

Roof a piazza of pigeons
who shat on his black Jeep.

His wife framed in the window with the baby going bye-bye.

My cold fingers untying the feeder string
Or useless in the garden all summer
drifting around with the radio on. The back stairs
get faded and wiggly, roses so leggy
they're all arms and thorns like a terrified woman.

She'd prune her big pink roses,
snipping and snapping at useless tendrils.

I tried not to glare, or fight. Why bother? Besides,
today the moving truck came.

So we come and go like this, watch each other
animated by fence slats.

THE SAVED

Continents called Mauritius
& so forth occurred.
Then we followed
a path to the river, down
into the river. In it people's
garments billowed & filled
with air and water as
someone pushed down
their heads like the muscles
of the birth canal & out
we staggered to lie gasping
and alone on the shore.

        Life, life, eternal life!

Bread, testicles, everything!
Clink clink go the wineglasses,
scrape scrape go the forks through
onions & carrots. Chattering
talking around the table in dreadful
brotherhood.

        Don't forget your hats and sunscreen!

Huge fat guys hunched
in the driver's seat taking forever
to turn a corner—forever predatory
we watch with our big eyes, big eye
teeth. Rump roast. Business proposition.

Pressed into witlessness yet
wishing something real would happen.

NEW HAMILTON WATCH 09/07/94

Teensy minute hand goes round & round
in shrunken circle

the dial of Being   gauges
machine pressure of
one Force or another, invisible,
impinging

like Spirit. I heard the Past Life
Regression Therapist on the radio say
"It's all energy
& energy never dies—"

She had been Guinevre. Insomnia cure
brought it out. I admired her confidence.

When one of her clients under hypnosis saw someone
crawling toward him saying "Louis the Fourteenth"
she said "look around, look down"—he does
& he's someone standing *beside* Louis
the Fourteenth!

I wonder who I was or whom
I stood beside. Every day in the mirror
it's like "who the heck
am I anyway?" Yet

I adapt. I poke the digits on the Speed Dial.
And when I tilt my new wristwatch
the numbers stretch & yawn.

LOUISE'S BRUSH

Louise pulls her brush out at Starbuck's—
"Excuse the hair" she says of a few
blond strands entwined in soft pale
bristles, back & handle palest dark cream—
from a shop in Ottawa her husband
frequents because they make such a fuss & wrap
things so fervently—we had our coffee
and a slice of matrimonial cake
and I was still innocent
of the romantic event that would follow
that very evening
when the stranger in the restaurant
would hand me a note about Rilke's poem
"The Swan"...

COLD SHOULDERS

Sponge dribbles hot
bathwater over shoulder-blades, one side,
other side, again and again in a trance—

Coolness finally assuaged, blade-sharpness
rounded and relaxed in the slump of bath-
posture—who cares?—and slump
farther into perfect heat—

The difficulty is finding the will
to get up out of it, to return & is
a bit like living. So I rub a space
into the fogged surface of the mirror,
finding myself there whole and large,
streaming water, strange bare animal
requiring a greeting.

DANGEROUS

A dangerous poem
camouflaged as a monkey.

A love poem a dangerous poem.

The poem of a monkey:
random & sincere:
smart monkey!

Faces nearly human
in the woods. Bodies
furred & furrowed brow
thinking in the forest—a
slight rise, a hillock
a good place for thinking.

How, possibly, to kill this
or that, or leave here,
leave her. Just
drive down to California, if
it takes all night you can pull
over, sleep, or not: just go.

Go be precious & perfect, find
your perfect anthem verse
where lions look up from the hot spill
of entrails & admire
the sight of the moon.

But it's too late, I'm, he's
old to be going anywhere else.
But sit here on its haunches
on the train to Alexandria
watching the sumac blur by
as a maroon haze in ditches
of broken stone & flexing branch.

22

TSUNAMI

The wave caught up
to all who ran
away from it,
tiny and afraid.

Curved at the top
like a gesture a hand makes
that wants to kill in jest
or the witch behind the tree—
black surprise, toppled bicycle
now riderless alas.

Stapled to existence
the wave draws near. Hands and feet
stick out of it. Debris
sluices along, voices call
for help, pieces of wet lumber,
chunks of spruce bark, sodden gyproc,
flung-away tires,
bear claw on a flash of chain.

THE HIT

Knocked out
by the lovingly-sketched biceps of a sky-
god out of the clear blue & pure white

While people walked along wearing black shoes
& pushing baby strollers. I say to myself
"Why don't you
go over to the island?" And why not
do this or that awful thing, why not
move to Helsinki, it's hell
sinking here without no
conversation & where I dwell
my only outlook

And what I faced in hell
neither furnace nor ice-crystal city
nor sour-faced aunts telling you
get in here now therefore I had to go inside
stand in the kitchen with the others
the frying fat odorous as attar
of roses. Gets in your sweater, your sweeter
cousin offering a game of Chinese checkers,
cold marbles set in cool tin perfect
depressions red & blue as the waffle-dips
of dragons whose backs sprout Gothic
darkening wings

Like Esther Williams' dive and crawl, her black
bathingsuit & red black lips my first movie,
her quick legs kicking the cousins crying
fishing beneath the seat for spilled Rosebuds.

BIOGRAPHY OF A WOMAN

She was so intelligent
she could see wind and hear
the coughing of flies,
in the basement she worried
about things that hadn't happened yet
but could, her suitors
were swans or had an arm
missing, she lost their engagement
rings, their car keys, was beaten,
shunned, kidnapped, she woke
in a deep well, fled & was captured,
forced to sort through ten tons
of millet pearl rice popcorn seeds
all night by haughty types who
tortured her with impunity, jealous
of her hair, her goodness that led
to betrothal and them snarky &
evil behind the curtain
as she stepped into the golden
crystal carriage but then she lost
the keys or spilled the wax or
dropped the stitch or found
a dwarf—was dropped off
in the woods at night & forced to sew
starlight into shirts enough
for an army, had her hands chopped off,
her feet removed, was mistaken for a broom
& left in a corner, she had to clean up
after devils and soldiers—
she was so intelligent she
was the chosen bride of the king's son
because she was so beautifully starved

that apples flung themselves off apple trees
into her grown-back hands at midnight.

MIDDEN LAYER, PRINCE GEORGE, c. 1962

Always night up north
when you did anything in town
after school. 3:00 the boyfriends
arrive in a regatta of idling cars & engine exhaust.
Their girlfriends hated school too. Grown women.
Just showed up, endured French and Geometry, left
at 3 with their lovers.

Smelled car leather, sweat,
spilled beer.
Baby Love
oh baby love we sang out
the open window. Wilderness
sat there.

Trees, road ahead, night sky,
black opening lake sudden
in the headlights. Rummaged
for cigarettes, mirror, our faces
were cameos, out in the bush, late summer,
Friday night.

Drivers exchange news, mythologies
of insane anonymous rage, stitches
at the hospital, the terrible stories
that were true floated through town.

Someone's father singing "Hold that Tiger!"
in the rec. room, another father
paces the house in a kilt
pressing with his underarm the bladder
of his bagpipes, a hokey broken wailing,
the slow procession of his feelings.

Dark out, white snow.

Speed skaters switch directions at the ice rink,
hot breath, cold metal of headgear,
bodies of iron and fire. All night beehive burners,
like suns, throw off nebulas
into the dark as the skaters swiftly pursue
the grace of a turn, quick
crossing motion of legs.

Ate beef & greens at midnight,
walked home past the dark library, the glass brick
liquor store a shiny temple in the moonlight,
past the radio station, the late night broadcaster
alone in the control room turning 45's
back & forth to find the beginning
of the actual music.

Moonlight, snow light, street light, headlight,
we were alone and never had to be wrestled from
chaperones, kisses stank of rye & Saturday

meant major damage and no one could help it.
The deejay cued up
& the bootleggers
answered the door, heard cops' questions,
got in the back seat, went downtown.

THE WELL

A stone circumference
cold & echoing
hoards the water
in the well. It sloshes
there, dark and quiet.
Its deep obsidian
reflects the lost look
on the face of the Girl
of the Limberlost who goes
there against her will, *beaten
& terrorized* into submission.
Well. She'll live, go on
with blue eyes, black hair
into the big city.

AFTERNOON WITH LIVER

Sunrise a thin scrap of cellophane
from out in the valley where the blue-
berries grow, I'm wide awake early & kind of
disappointed in homeopathy

Later the ceasing
of the rain and a mildness
extends itself & holds me as I walk
through fragile groups of mourners
at the Gospel Chapel on the way
to the meat market where the butcher's
apprentice hauls a plastic bag of
liver from the cooler

& spills it out onto a wide wooden block
where it unfolds like the universe,
finding its own shape & equilibrium—
a little narrower at one end,
a gloss of winter starlight hugging the rise
at the other end

and with newly practised grace he sliced off
a portion for the display case dark red
& full of vitamins and angled the rest
back into the bag. Boy oh boy, I thought.

My hat was off to that particular cow.

THE BROKEN CUP
(terza rima)

Bits of prosody fall near what remains of me
that drifts on the sofa in a trance
made of loves, lazy rivers, unmended crockery.

I feel so broken now by a too-long dance.
Shot exhausted horses fall behind the stadium
and shards of mirror lance

What could have been a fatal wound, fatal tedium
or a spiritual lesson to have learned
endlessly postponed like closure & delirium.

One wants clear endings, beginnings to burn
big holes through old obdurate patterns, one wants
love to "triumph" as it were but not to earn

A thousand bardos, a daily headache, an ounce
of comfrey for a cure when I am acting up
& slink around ashamed of getting trounced

At life & coping, nearly. Like certain music
refuses transcendence (that strange vulgarity),
and how I threw the broken cup

Away because I know to hope for clarity
where things are broken is just to lie.

DAY WITH NOVOCAINE

The shadow of a gull crosses Broadway from south to north
the centre line hops over the rim of the world
third gear, green lights turn me into the Elect
near noon people in tank tops wait at the crosswalk
wait for me to go by first
before stepping out to cross the hot expanse
so drugged I love them, their babies slumped in strollers
holding formula bottles straight up in the air
I love them but not enough to stop for them
the ride is so smooth, the way paved with gold &
the tires filled with air
no one back of me, no one in front
the rear view mirror holds the mortal world
slightly smoked, I'm loping
toward the future, toward instructional videos
empty urgent blinking screens
sedated, happy, warm in the hot black insides
of the car, my face paralyzed as a gangster's,
mind cool, hands steady, tinted glass
keeping out the wind, the cruel puffs of cold air
they puff & puff on your back teeth to find out
which one needs the attention

LATE SUMMER

Snapdragons—
pink and silver voices—
sun late to go—
someone plunking out
Mood Indigo—

Sweet time
of honey and sunflower, Byzantine
light through the sprinklers—

& meanings, for sure.

POND & HORSES

Two huge sisters get into a blue sedan,
the sedan sinks & we're next at the pump, fire
ripping through the valley & the subdivisions. So,
we got there. A horse called Charlie bites
an old red truck & wind-chime rods bang
& fly at each other like a bunch of maniacs. Charlie
muddies the pond, Charlie at loose ends
with a hard-on in the yard

The graceful other horse is ridden by the girl's posture
whereas I sink
in the saddle and am utterly destroyed
by love, a French novel

Minus the nude argument scenes. I like
Charlie's huge eye on this side and on that side *mesembria*
the parting in his mane, X hands high a human measure
to buy flowers for the dead & decorate an altar:
where do they go? Everyone
small and brief on folding chairs in the auditorium
watching the flute player pass his breath past grabbing holes.
The idea is to be the same as nature
but we're not—
green star, yellow flower, bee or butter
shadow on our cheeks laid there by sweetness, the living
with people we barely knew but got along with I suppose

As horses neckwise know & care each for each behind the fence
they could leap but don't & stand there sleeping
in the wind & pine-smoke on their lucky feet.

THE LIBRARY

The book I had wanted to borrow
under the category
"autobiographical fiction"
was in the bindery

How long? I asked
the librarian.
Five or six months
she said.

But it could be sooner,
you never know.

Meantime I couldn't shake
the dream I'd had last night
about moving
to a new house.

89 W. 89th
14 W. 14th
10 W. 10th
22 W. 22nd

It had an address
something like that.
In the back yard
was a community

And the neighbourhood was called "Belle"
as in "La Belle et la Bête."
As usual, my husband
was ignoring me

Though he never ignores me
in real life. See you later
he said as he closed
the car door

And I went on north
toward town. Parking
cost me 5 quarters.
It was Day Two of the GST.

People were all excited about it,
outraged confused.

Clerks tied themselves up in explanations.

When I'm old I too will be oblivious to the steam
& length of the line-up behind me.

THE WATERMELON

The clock said l0 to 3.

I went upstairs, wrote lines, crossed them out.

I felt the weight of one of those gas masks on my spirit.

"My spirit." My size 7 1/2 shoe.
My Canada Life insurance policy.

I suppose this comes from the pain of living, which is
like being stabbed.

Everywhere I look,
books.

I suppose Sharon Olds has just finished another
fabulous poem about her child's scalp.

Poetry: I couldn't care less.

Long lines, short lines:
two ways of suffocation.

Head down, knitting a black garment.

It won't yield. The current stops.
Thought loops back on itself, knots
tight as a tourniquet.

Stories laugh at me.

I picked up the phone.

I wrote the alphabet. Then I printed it.

Last night's dream drifts around
like colored smoke.

I've always loved rivers. Music.

Thoughts, sayings, about what goes on.
What I hear and think I know. It's saying
"That's the demon that nearly jumps out at you."

Poetry makes me feel like getting drunk. I wish
I was a man.

If I was someone else, would I prefer
their troubles to my own?

I would wash my face, brush my teeth, etc. reach for briefcase
open at the top with some xeroxing sticking out.

There's nothing Southern about me.

AGREEMENT

Each of the cold sandwiches is
not are. The ditto machine concurs,
alcohol damp purple instructions
wafting to a tray. Will
flies in and out with voice mail
in his hands.

In my office I was in Mexico
enduring my identity.

It wouldn't matter he's the same
age as my father. That we stood
on a beach never alone. That
there was a sense of rightness:
my perpetual perplexity.

MEANWHILE

Tulip petals shrivel to dark lilies.

The piano chokes on a wire.

Plants bury a relative, a bird

frightens the mirror. The cat

crouches in the litter box &

the kingdom trembles, angora floating

in the furnace breeze joining eternity.

Ice cubes assume crystals. Returning

I turn on lamps & dash through subtle patterns

arranged by insects. Sky falls with

water, dark border takes me over.

INSOMNIA

Do something hard
as tires one out
by 7:30, ready
to hit the hay

At sundown.
All through the dark
how soft a sighing
the wind makes!

Then sunrise
—a subtle
slow change in the hue
of the pillow-case.

BILLIE HOLIDAY'S NYLONS

                                        hospital window

                        smokey mountains

42

            smoky halo, hair pulled tight

                quick

brass smack   light wrists

crossed on white pillow in moonlight through

a little moonlight and you through

the windowsill's

                ashtray hairpins vodka *wolf willow*

                                    big body's nod toward them

                    caught & led, or leading

come over here   trousers drape the chair-back

                lifts her head

to the sip   stripped

    of her dangerous

            & door locked & inventory:

green comb, toothbrush, Joy by Patou, other brassiere, mink stole,   *43*

checkbook, insurance forms   what a little moonlight

      can do anything

  the fountain flows over its rim onto vistas

she they hauntedness sang out   dragging back behind the beat

smoke in the air round her head

        deep gardenia, cool heavy microphone

fountain body   come over here   need for you is

worsen just bad

    in the castle hospital

   stone casements, guarded doors, men handsome & kind

      turn her beauty

         high-drape pants over

   chair back, suspender

nooses loop down

                        gather up   the overflow

AFTER ROY KIYOOKA'S FUNERAL

I take a kitchen chair out to the front porch
and stand on it to reach the light.
Encased in amber bubbled
glass, which has to be unscrewed
in three small places. The screws are brass,
stiff, unused to suffering. Then the
40 watt bulb comes out and in goes
a 100 watt bulb. The amber casing
back on, with its old cheap bracing
screws. Now
my visitors. Now the path
is lit farther out—and
the way in brighter,
bigger.

ROSE WINDOW

Here comes summer, a red
truck. A friend of yours,
maybe?

And who did you say you are, again.

I am the Japanese poet
who missed the ferry to Galiano
and had to sit in plastic chairs
for three hours.

Trying to remember
a cassoulet I had in Toulouse
& the cathedral there, Romanesque

So tomorrow it will be this or that
in the usual order—some visitors
or maybe drive somewhere.
Or maybe no visitors.

So they arrived. The smallest
child (a) fell down
and banged his forehead (b)
picked a lethal mushroom
(c) trampled the tall grasses
we were growing for hula skirts

Then he lifted weights,
his little arms trembling.

Go ahead. Do everything
your heart desires. Just remember,

I'll still be around.

Even though at Jake's I had toast and coffee
and forgot to pay & Diana
wondered if I had any erotica.

My erotica my petunia.

Fruit of the womb whose entrance-way folds like
the alabaster praying hands of the Virgin
crowning the altar. At Chartres, stony
windowed hollow, jewel-toned spacecraft,
rock jar, treasure cave.

The books, the bones
are hidden. Flesh house.

Whose surrounding decorative grasses are squashed
by prone figures of little children
raising and lowering their arms
being birds, pilots, angels, daredevils,
flying buttresses.

Out of desperation, boredom, out of
the panic of trying to be good.

Four years old & the mind of a supervisor.

THE HEY DIDDLE DIDDLE FRIEZE

There's a plate with legs wearing shoes
a sleepy moon reclining
night-cap and pink pompom

With yellow horns the cow
dangles her udder
where dogs laugh amongst the stars

So hard they are tickled pink
on the floor clutching their ribs

At the plate walking by

No wonder babies cry
in such a room
to grow up notwithstanding
the mother and the night-light

she dims the better to see
the shining moon alone
anointing the back yard, black ovals
of bush cupping
the endless excuses

& broken hearts all over again

as dish and spoon run off together
in large pastel shoes.

CHICAGO, O'HARE AIRPORT, TERMINAL ONE

I was asked to put my seatback tray
in the upright position for landing.
So I did.

Crumpled black mountains below, lakes tilting,
all that stuff, who cares. Nervously

I remember I paid $10 to a fortune teller
who told me I'd suffered
many disappointments.

True, I have.

Another $10 she'd do the cards.

Pinwheel-colored lightning roams
the ceiling over the people conveyed
by moving walkways & delivered
to the gates.

In somnolent doomsday tones
the announcement is repeated:
please look down the moving walkway is ending

We look down.

We like to do as mother says,
perhaps she will offer us her breast.

On the perfectly pressed uniforms
of the higher-ups floating toward us
are brooches consisting of metal wings.

50

My fortune said I would be happy again
the following year.

It was true, I was.

THE PARROT

She flew, she was up
& gone, they had let her out
for a treat & were sorry now.
Red tail feathers
way, way up in a fir tree
on the side of a mountain.
It was north. Crows
eyed her. Way, way down
the people were making
little pyramids of peanuts &
calling her name: Isabel! Isabel!
They clicked their tongues
and whistled, they went away and
came back later. The sun got large
and red, turned the heat up
under her vocabulary. Later
they could hear her exhortations
to the moonlight: Hey Sailor!
Good Golly Miss Molly! Want
A Cracker? So What!
The crows backed off
& stared, diamond bracelets dangling
from their beaks. All that night
the parrot prayed & sang,
in the morning it was over.
She glided downward, branch
to spiky branch. The people
wept and applauded, rushed her
back to her cage exhausted,
the undisputed champion
of the air. She was never the same
after that. The vet said it was

a bit like the cave scene
in *A Passage to India*—something
to do with language, the dark &
existence. Stupendous!
the parrot kept saying for years
after & the crows invented a dream.

EATING SMARTIES IN THE TRUCK

City hoves in, rank fields soak
diesel & manure, nothing grows,
what shall we eat, corn from Illinois,
sambas from Japan, diamond bracelet
in the bank vault, three yellow Smarties,
the happiness of the world when
that man asks that woman to dance
& she puts her cigarette out firmly
and right away. Gets up taller. Him too.
She's a little drunk, which is scandalous,
but just a little drunk, a little scandalous.
So is he, or he wouldn't have asked her.
I was alive and watching. I had eaten
nachos. My scarf was decorated with
the leaning tower of Pisa. Women were
getting up and singing & one clutched the mike
with a silk gardenia in her hair. The emcee
was manic and the trumpet player
blew at the floor, sadly and thinly,
no matter the song. It was snowing outside
and the orange plow came by shaking the earth, pushing
snow out of the way with a great blade.
How everything forms
& you never know until later what was just
ahead. Deas Island tunnel, traffic converging
on the Oak Street Bridge, coming up from
the States. Couldn't stand
what was on the radio & felt around inside
the nearly empty Smarties box with a free hand.
I miss the sight of his man's knees beside me,
each breadth of them under the dashboard
so bony and goodnatured.

VALENTINE

Once out of Yeats I can breathe
and every tatter on its singing branch.

Snipping the shoulder pads
out of everything, a mound
of mute foam forms.

In the front row sits pale Lily
and even paler Grace.

At a certain age one is flattered
by earrings that look like teeth.

When we met we looked sideways.

I was happy to tell him
the story of my hair—a long
story involving an elevator.

What a tale! And what
wolfy eyes you have!

French was still in my tongue,
a slight pressure toward the lips,
a certain esprit in the scarf
at my throat—towers tipping in Pisa,
labyrinths and thick spirals.

It was a lot but I got it
thirty percent off.

I heated milk, bubbled

the espresso pot: life,
life, eternal life!

Until the time came I
wasn't thinking anything except
to extend an acquaintance past dark.

Tequila I replied. But they didn't have any.

There was snow on the ground, I saw
the orange plow go by like an ocean liner
with its head up.

The tremble. It reaches you.

SPUTNIK MEASURES

When you force listening
down it's all there.
The bird cheep. The traffic. Agitated
clarinet on the radio a moment ago
switched off suddenly angrily. Big shot
control panel. So like
a satellite she tears around
the outer darkness of his planet-
centrism, translating
pathways of storms—cloudy
spirals intentioned as a herd of bees
among a mass of blue
hollyhocks—from a distance. She has
many books to read, one
on what gardens can't help meaning. Eventually
she will fall & all her data
with her. The EKG wire still attached
to her heart or wherever it is
attached. Navy divers will retrieve her from
the Indian Ocean—
she'll get to borrow one of them's
bathrobe. And then they'll
give her a certificate and a
brooch with a comet tail on it
made of gold & a strip of pink ruby.

WAITING FOR TELESCOPE TIME

Astronomers on "Ideas" carp re. the immovable
hegemony of the theoretical while people line up
just to look through the telescope, a carnival
glimpse at what's out there—jewellery probably—
dangling amongst the loose various gossamers
of her deshabille—*young bright stars* plus
Saturn with glitter scarf yanked round his throat,
old musician tired of itineraries
& the good folks of every city's happiness—

The otherwise mostly hopeless astronomers &
lonesome denizens of the Milky Way stir like women
stirring good soup a fire-blackened cauldron's
starry distillate. They
wear alpaca overcoats and at 75 elegantly know
how to bargain for the ineffable.

ON FIRST WATCHING "HONEYMOON IN VEGAS"

A comedy, therefore
persons falling in holes. Vexatious
Elvis convention. Wealthy geezer
Pluto-like hustles the hero's girlfriend
into a black limousine poised curbside
with burly attendants. And she
having sunned by the pool in white Spandex
is a teacher of small children, jeez,
a brain too, as he tots up
her charms. The plot

exasperates. Mt. Kiluaea blows up
spewing lava sparks at the astronomical night
& threatening the merry-makers of history
drinking and screwing in their beautiful
cities. Comedies

do that, you weep
with relief even knowing the ending
since Day One. No use believing
that just because you're happy you can
leave your good-luck charm on the blanket.
Or otherwise disconnect
from the ludicrous griefs
of persons betrayed & just go
snorkelling. The shrubbery might be a disguise,

a wall may speak. Falling Elvises may puncture
the night sky, their bodies outlined in flashing
lightbulbs. Each
has the same hairdo a bit askew, silver
studs on their white pants hot as meteorites.

AURORA

Garland remains of the starry dynamo surround her

Galactic waterfall shreds & threads over stone

And stone steep downward, the many kilowatts

feed cities, farms, basement operations.

Get the generator going. Fan blades churn a

Cumulus build-up, lights on, elevator up & down,

Everyone tied to phone or link. The risen cities

Of human splendor, cozy lounge, agencies,

Dog obedience school where two fall in love but there

Are complications not insurmountable, he has tinnitus

She's married eventually they'll join forces

Meantime our Queen beautiful and thrilling

Commanding both pipeline and angels

Evincing wrath at the fleeing night

Aswarm in garlands and little babies, prancing horses

Gilded wheels disperse the dark cumulus the hideous nightmare

The lying awake alone with sore tooth, so beautiful

The beginning of days brightening!

gala roses

62

If it's not flowing I'll not tell

not to ask me neither under the lilac nor upon the bedspread

a secret fig green orb a mouth the size fills

inside perfectly & juice a slight muscular taking

a trout in the boat under the sun's

tremor the sly slight feather the fisherman strokes

words upon you oh body oh stone lintel and maiden frieze

lifting high the garland gala roses white lilies

legs draped heavy satin skirting heads crowned braided

sung & caught by nets your sheer wings beauty

her gateway fig-mouth and trout so slips down

63

Was fast the shift to blankness the nape of neck's

adorable space many catastrophes could & have befallen

axes have fallen upon fair bent heads still speaking

don't think about it don't listen the dog is advised re

the nature of his operation & moans of pity no no

refuse to be bitter neither will he nor she all

friends & happy in the skin of some accommodation stretched

beyond bearing goes loose in the mind—covered saintlike

in arrows walking to work not screaming not yelling a kind word

the mailman the butcher the old woman rambling alone book in hand

kerchief & housedress a pocketful of amethysts & quartz crystal

Orange silk triangles shine from the berber kelim

green & blue oasis water sweetness pregnant moon adrift

large above the stucco the pointed rooflines grave

& magnificent occasions *it feels so good* entwined you my

darling my sweetheart the years each one lost to us

added on to sorrow's sad amazed boat nudging nudging

the wharf's oily edge blackened posts wavering

moon-blackened water's profound & frightful mirror

led here by what sure footedness *quietness & passion*

with or without him it them you see you big whatevers

going in and out like breathing I can't help it

Form follows whitely next the big tree shaded

fruitless not full of speeches like King Lear apoplectic

upholstered beneath the tent of his rent sub-

conscious we read as libretto to folly & lust

virtue's adventure high above nodding

here there to them below dirty-faced with cockney spraddle

good sense good rhymes or not-bad chocolate bar

some poor guy had to leave during the storm scene

passing knees in near tears mine also that people

idiotic in castles' granite chill behind the unicorns

draperies & trumpets strumpets waggle hips

blue skirts the young princes point at

Sour cream egg whites coconut icing sugar mountainous

sweetness missing the book of favorites my lord and saviour

wants me for a sunbeam others too but I sing me he wants me

eyebeams coiled on the violets river-bank pregnant

by mandrake root or thought *two hearts two hearts that beat*

as one covered over the site with leaf mould undid the night

pointed the way down the aisle's little footpath lites

two fingers each hand point to the exits existence outside

jumping into heaven's thought clouds blue peace cold wind

floating throne river of stars the big lap

and book the white chest, odor of father comes now

Illumination marches thoughtless around in shorts

watch out where youre going map turned this way

that way north switched to south

ㅤㅤ:ed round to north again whacked

ㅤㅤ:ourse *within human memory* velikovsky imagines venus

came so close she threw the earth off its spinning

broke necks with suddenness massive reversals hence

concussive reeling waters slop beehives coil whales dive

ant colony exudes itself a grayish pile by the roadside's

hairpin turn lake blasting blue & huge mountainous cold

planet of *seas and vapors, mud, fire, and dust*

Red head of rose partitions the vase lip

he gave me relaxed on the porch charming bare

arm offering sweet muscles long curve I'll take

too then taking took mine so entwined twinned arms oh

well the picnic today so fry chicken all morning

dip egg dip crumbs lay down in the brilliant cooking

ocean floating things persons dog paddling

old & sandy muzzled sneezing wagging creature full

moon moaning through clouds & trees she chants

the puzzle of the blessed virgins virginity but

things do happen emma laraine's daughter smiling due november

Triste tropiques bristle of boat stems at the yacht club

ocean sways round turquoise peaks long as Indonesia

tips obscured toes dipped in the sea for a feeling of *out*

there we made it to maybe we'll go somewhere we'll

70

be okay as of this day at the park looking

for a familiar posture or hair or gesture on the green

nice to see so many families jungle gyms hibachi smoke

weather-talk clouds clearing the breaking in two

and into twos the coil of something—helpless resemblance

& architecture of long forgotten desire remaining an *indepth*

report HELP ME bottle bobbing its message too late probably

Hammering fixes looseness plunging the wayward turd

sunshine neck-rash heat flush orgone headache gap-tooth

concealed smile invites the neighbour for tea just over

the flu finally ready to cope with the white hydrangea

purchase to clamber around the house-front a viney apron

I hide my face in boo-hoo I cry mother pats me

there there fixing sheets to the line hot & windy dark hair

blowing & out the car window us in the back or

over by the gas station long weeds tight

budded yellow flowers red rocket tips pale violet surrender

to who's responsible who picks it up and runs with it

Tone is something to take in the lake whose arms

embrace peninsulas of trees teepees canoes and strings

of hung smoked fishes all in the museum The Museum

of Love and of What Is Pretty, purchases from abroad *foreign*

merchandise sd the American grandma from her wing chair 93

pushed the plate-glass door to the early bird sitting

open herself expecting to find things

not to her liking: the tune on the player piano.

On her dictionary flyleaf in blue ink *nostalgia*

arthritis recluse royal expanse of lawn out the window

should have been peacocks too but their cries hurt she

never stopped loving her third husband the one

who looked like Spencer Tracy

Green machine beyond the ruby dahlias & empty

town without you-him-it a gap thinking fills overflows

scrolled as music coiling out the mouth of the alto

love's refrain ornamented elizabethan *garden*

wall where stars are bright imagination hides her purple

violets *such sweet sorrow* striates the mind like bar codes

dragged over a dark star a price appearing or someone

at the door with a seven-rap tattoo shave-and-a-haircut

the drag queens' audience drab by the default's wild

fuschia gloves silver gowns mountainous Bo-peep wigs

the gallantry stiff shoulders and exaggerated mouth of her

continuous birth

big dipper's steam shovel

permanently on strike zenith of summer summit of green &

breezes the Queen is here walking along the rows

of soldiers chests or in a late-model convertible we hold

74

to her civet cat robes & make petitions to keep

to life and love the living and dear God I cried

bring him back on my knees on stones of the earth some birds

at it in the ripening plum tree the sun out oh Christ

I cried & arose the day as usual bright & fractious

sweet juices jamming the beaks of the crows &

their ancient nightsome noisome

Accorded the morning its habit & rhythm, rain clouds

kitty litter *little things that drive you crazy* whining

race cars round the stadium going nowhere unhelpful

attachments of the vacuum cleaner hose uncoiling

the one with the headlamp that roars & grabs at the rug

fallen dahlia petals white paper dots from the 3-hole punch

waiting for him to come & the courier also & also her what if

they come while you're out & miss the rap the doorbell

messenger in uniform his parcel his brown truck & quickness

just in case bring out the blue & white cups blue & white saucers

gala of milky breasts pouring a funnel of stars and

rain on my ornamental plum

Sharon Thesen is a Vancouver poet and editor. Her selected poems, *The Pangs of Sunday*, was published by McClelland and Stewart in 1990. Coach House Press has published three of her books of poetry: *Artemis Hates Romance*, *Holding the Pose* and *The Beginning of the Long Dash* (nominated for the Governor-General's Award in 1987). She edited *The New Long Poem Anthology* (Coach House Press, 1991).

Editor for the Press: Michael Redhill
Cover Illustration: Guido Reni, detail from *Aurora* (1613), fresco.
Cover Design: Pippa White
Author photograph: Jonas Papaurelis

Coach House Press
50 Prince Arthur Avenue, Suite 107
Toronto, Canada   M5R 1B5